10-23-1
25.00

Gr 3-6

890L

INFO WISE

RESEARCH
AND
SYNTHESIZE
YOUR
FACTS

~Valerie Bodden~

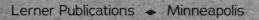

Lerner Publications ◆ Minneapolis

For Josh and our little projects—Hannah, Elijah, Titus, and Chloe

Lerner Publications Company
A division of Lerner Publishing Group, Inc.
241 First Avenue North
Minneapolis, MN 55401 USA

For reading levels and more information, look up this title at www.lernerbooks.com.

Main body text set in Adrianna Regular 11/18. Typeface provided by Chank.

The Cataloging-in-Publication Data for *Research and Synthesize Your Facts* is on file at the Library of Congress.
    ISBN 978-1-4677-5224-4 (LB)
    ISBN 978-1-4677-7581-6 (PB)
    ISBN 978-1-4677-6231-1 (EB pdf)

Manufactured in the United States of America
1 — CG —12/31/14

3 4873 00513 4564

CONTENTS

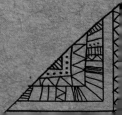

INTRODUCTION

TIME TO GET ORGANIZED

So you're working on a research project. And you're feeling pretty good about your progress. You've done all the preliminary stuff—choosing a topic and coming up with research questions. You've even tracked down a bunch of sources and picked out the ones you're going to use. Now you need to do something with them. But what? Should you just spread them out on your desk and start writing your paper? Whoa, hold on! You almost missed a step.

You need to spend some quality time with those sources before you can start writing. You need to read them, think about them, and take notes on the relevant information in them. Then you need to shuffle and sort those notes into a clear outline.

It seems like a lot of work, doesn't it? That's because it is! You will likely spend more time on this step than on any other part of your research project. But all that work will pay off when it's finally time to write your paper, because you'll have everything in place. Pull out your note cards and your first source, and let's get started!

CHAPTER 1

THE NOTETAKER'S TOOL KIT

Before you jump into taking notes, you have to decide what note-taking method you will use. *Why do I need a method?* you ask. *Can't I just start writing or typing?* Remember, your goal is to organize your information so that you can find it later. You may be able to find things in your room even when it's a mess, but the same is not necessarily true of your notes. If you choose a good note-taking system and stick to it, your whole project will go more smoothly.

INDEX CARDS

Your teacher may require you to take notes on index cards. *Ugh*, you may be thinking, *so old school.* But this tried-and-true method has plenty of pluses. You can only fit a limited amount of information on an index card, which will help you break big ideas into small, manageable chunks. And index cards are easy to shuffle and rearrange. That will help you get your information organized when you write your outline.

If you use index cards, write down only one idea per card—one fact, one statistic, one quote, one example, or one expert's opinion. If you write too much information on one card, you might run into problems later, when you want to sort your cards. What if you want to use one point from the card in the first paragraph of your paper, but you want to use another point somewhere else? Short of cutting your cards apart or rewriting them, you're going to have a problem. So save yourself some hassle and stick to one idea per card!

Label each card with the last name of the source's author. If no author is given, list the title instead. If you have more than one source by the same author, include at least part of the title too so you know which one the note came from. If you're using a print source, list the page number where you found this piece of information. (An online source probably won't have page numbers, so you're off the hook there.)

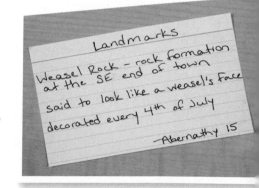

Why go to all this trouble to keep track of where your notes came from? Well, it makes things easier for you. If you need to double-check the note later, you'll know where to look. And you'll need this information to cite your sources in your paper—you don't want to have to hunt all over for it when it's time to write.

Most of your information will likely fall into smaller categories within your overall topic. So label each note with a subject heading too. Each subject heading will stand for a different category, or subtopic. For example, if you are researching your hometown, you might label some cards "history," some "landmarks," and some "important people."

NOTEBOOKS

Not a fan of index cards? You might choose to take notes in a notebook instead—as long as your teacher is OK with that. Notes in a notebook are not as easy to rearrange, but a notebook gives you more room to write your own ideas alongside the notes you take.

You can dedicate specific pages (or a separate notebook) to each subtopic you're researching. So if you're writing about solar eclipses, you might use one notebook page for notes about the science behind solar eclipses. Another page might be reserved for notes about mythical explanations of eclipses. Just like with index cards, be sure to write the last name of the source's author (or the title if no author is given) after each note, along with a page number. Your notes will probably be easier to read if you skip a line between each entry.

The downside of this method is that you'll have to do a lot of page turning. Say you're reading an article about Sacagawea's role in the Lewis and Clark expedition. You might take notes in the categories "cultural background," "early life," "work as interpreter," and "other skills and activities." That means you'll constantly be flipping through your notebook to find the right spot for each type of note. The upside, though, is that you'll be organizing your notes as you go along. It'll save you time later.

If you think all that page-flipping will slow you down too much, you can split up your notes by source instead of by subtopic. Start a new notebook page for each source you use. List the source's information at the

"History of Wibbly wob Candy," Kidd

2 candy company started by Robert "Wob" Wibblerforce in 1903

2 first candy type too slippery to eat

2 second version more solid, but storage still a problem

3 "ongoing problems arising from its ability to bend the space-time continuum"

5 Wob's son, Merlin, took over the company in 1930

5-6 "Sales dropped during the Great Depression" —but people tried to steal the candy for "its supposed ability to reshape time" —lots of sad songs written about people down on their luck with no Wibbly wobs to change their fate

top of the page. Then write down all your notes from that source. This way, you don't have to write the source's name at the end of each note. But you should still write down page numbers if your source has them. Label each note with a subject heading too. Try using a different colored highlighter or marker to mark each subject heading. When you go back through your notes later, you'll have an easier time spotting which notes are related by subject.

DIGITAL DETAILS

Does the thought of writing all those notes by hand make your fingers curl? If your teacher allows it, you can try taking notes on a computer instead. Just be sure to save your work!

You can start with a blank computer document. Make separate pages (or even separate files) for each subject heading or each source. Later, you'll be able to copy and paste your notes into groupings by subject. Or you can make a spreadsheet for your notes. Use the first column to list the subject of each note, and then type your note in the next column. Use the third column to keep track of source information. When you're done taking notes, just sort them by the subject column, and—*voilà!*—all the notes about each subject will automatically be grouped together.

Whichever method you choose, you'll likely get the hang of it quickly. Soon you'll have a stack of index cards, a full notebook, or a giant spreadsheet. And what kind of information should be in these notes? That's the next challenge in your research quest.

CHAPTER 2

TAKE NOTE OF IT

Once you've decided *how* to write your notes, you need to decide *what* to write. Maybe you're thinking you have a superb memory, so you need to write down only a few things. You'll just remember the rest. There are two problems with that strategy. First, you might be able to remember that there are 360,000 species of beetles in the world, but can you also remember what they eat, how long they live, their range of sizes, and which species don't have wings? Probably not—especially if you also have to remember what's happening in your other classes, not to mention the rest of your life. Second, you don't just need to remember the facts you'll be using. You need to be able to show your readers where you found them. So thorough note-taking is a must.

Does that mean you should make notes on *everything* you read? After all, if it was important enough to be included in your source, it's important enough to write down, right? Not necessarily.

Not everything in every source is going to be relevant to your topic or help you prove your thesis. For example, it might be interesting that the average American throws away 4.3 pounds (2 kilograms) of garbage a day, but that doesn't mean it's related to your report on air pollution.

Think about the list of research questions you wrote way back at the beginning of your project, before you even began digging for sources. (What's that? You didn't write any research questions? Well, there's no time like the present. Make a list of questions related to your project's topic that you want to answer through your research.) Whenever you come across a fact in your sources that answers one of your research questions—even if it's just a partial answer—write it down. You may also find a fact that answers a question you hadn't even thought of but that you want to include in your project. Write that down too. And add the new question to your list!

Are statistics about garbage collection relevant to your report on air pollution? If not, no need to include them in your notes.

You can also take notes on any background information that will make the topic easier for you and your readers to understand. For instance, if you're researching the Boston Tea Party of 1773, you might take notes on the Tea Act, the law that sparked this protest.

TYPES OF NOTES

You've found something you think you should write down. But should you write it in your own words? Or should you copy it word for word from the source? That depends. Let's talk about the three main types of notes you can take.

If you want to use just a few words to capture the main idea of a paragraph, a chapter, or even a complete work, you can make a summary note. For example, a summary note about this book might go something like this: *Before you begin to write, you need to take notes, track your sources, and make an outline.* Notice that a summary does not include specific details. Instead, it gives a general overview. This type of note can be useful if you want to sum up an author's position on a topic. But make sure that your summary reflects the author's overall view—not just one part of it. Say for instance that an author supports the use of robots as restaurant servers. In one section of her article, she mentions possible problems that robot servers could cause. It would not be accurate to summarize the article as *opposing* the use of robot servers just because of that section.

Another type of note-taking is paraphrasing. Unlike summarizing, paraphrasing focuses on specific information in the source. When you paraphrase, you rewrite the author's ideas in your own words. The goal is to capture the author's point without copying the author's exact words or phrasing. Maybe your source says, "Although vending machines bring schools needed funding, that money is not worth the risk to students' health." You might paraphrase it like this: *Schools put students' health at risk by allowing vending machines in their buildings in return for money.* Of course, these notes don't have to be in complete sentences. You can use abbreviations or your own shorthand to make note-taking faster and easier. So you might paraphrase the source about vending machines with a shorthand note like this:

vending machines
pro = money for schools
con = health risks to students

Just make sure not to go overboard. You want to be able to understand your notes later! A super-short note like *VM: +$$, - h* may not make much sense to you two days down the road.

Your final note-taking option is the quotation. When you write a quotation note, you copy a source's exact words. You might do this if you think something in the source is particularly well stated. Or you might want to quote the words of a historical figure or a primary source such as a novel. Sometimes quoting an expert can be the easiest way to explain a point. It can also make your argument more convincing. In some cases, you might even quote someone who disagrees with you, just to make sure that you express his views fairly.

Put quotation marks around anything you copy directly from your sources. That way, when you look over all your notes again later, you'll know for sure which notes are your own words and which are your sources' words. And don't use abbreviations or shorthand when writing down quotes. You don't want to risk misquoting a source when you write your paper.

If you want to use only part of a quote, you can leave some words out. Indicate the omission with an ellipsis (three periods).

Suppose a source says, "Wearing a bike helmet will not protect you from all harm, but it will reduce the risk of head injury." You could shorten the quote to look like this: "Wearing a bike helmet . . . will reduce the risk of head injury." Just make sure that deleting parts of the quote doesn't change its meaning. For example, if your source says, "I do not believe in aliens," you can't use an ellipsis to remove "not": "I do . . . believe in aliens." In this case, you've made the quote mean the opposite of what your source said.

Are you researching the safety benefits of bike helmets? You may want to quote an expert's opinion.

Don't worry about using the "wrong" type of note. Just because you record a quotation doesn't mean you have to use it in your final project. You might decide to paraphrase that idea instead. Or you might not include the idea at all. But at least you have the quote if you want it. It can work the other way too.

Say you paraphrased an idea, but when you start working on your paper, you decide that you'd rather quote this source. You're in luck! See how your note lists the author of the source you used, plus the page number? Just grab that source and flip to that page—or type that website address into your search engine. You'll find your quote in seconds.

FACT VS. OPINION

Once you're on a roll with note-taking, it's easy to get caught up in capturing information. But don't forget to think as you research. Pay attention to whether what you're writing down is a fact or an opinion. You probably already know that a fact is something that can be proven and an opinion is based on one person's (or a group of people's) beliefs. *George Washington was our nation's first president* is a fact. *George Washington was our nation's best president* is an opinion.

Both facts and opinions can help you build on your thesis. Facts can offer concrete evidence to support your point. But often the same facts can be interpreted in different ways. That's where opinion comes in. Of course, your paper will reflect your own opinions—your take on the facts. But it should also include the opinions of experts on your topic. These opinions will add credibility to your argument.

Sorting through facts and opinions as you research can be confusing. Perhaps the results of a scientific study convinced a group of scientists that human settlement on Mars will be possible within thirty years. But another group of scientists looking at the same study concluded that a Martian settlement could never work. Meanwhile, a completely different study convinced a third group of scientists that Mars *can* be settled—but not for another fifty years. How do you know what to write down? For now, write down all three arguments. You might later decide to include them all in your paper. Or you might find other sources that strongly support one group's conclusion.

An artist drew this sketch of possible colonies on Mars. Look for additional sources to decide if this concept is based on facts or opinions.

Try to find more than one reliable source for each fact. You don't necessarily need to make the same note twice, though. Instead, you can find the card with the original note on it and add the new source's information at the bottom of it. Now you'll remember that those two sources agree—and your argument will be that much stronger.

But what if you find some information that contradicts the point you're trying to make? Should you ignore it? Nope! Write that down too. This is extra important if you're working on a persuasive paper. One of the ways to make your point is to discuss opposing arguments—and why you disagree with them.

THINK BIG PICTURE

As you research, keep your larger goal in mind. At some point, you're going to need to put together a paper that combines your own thoughts with your sources' information. So start analyzing how you feel about the information you're finding.

Even as you're making notes from your sources, add some personal notes too. These notes can contain your opinions about the research you are doing. For example, maybe you're reading in your sources that violent video games have been linked to increases in bullying. Your reaction might be this: "How can researchers be sure that the video game violence led directly to bullying? Maybe kids who are naturally more violent are more likely to play violent video games. So maybe the link actually works the other way around." You can use this thought as a jumping-off point for more research. You might find sources that explore the same idea. But meanwhile, always label your personal notes so you know that they came from you and not from any other source.

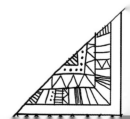

CHAPTER 3

SOURCES, SOURCES EVERYWHERE

What's a researcher's worst nightmare? It might go like this. You've returned all your books to the library and closed all your browser tabs. But you realize you need to double-check some information. You look at the label for one of your notes. All you have to go on is the author's last name: Smith. So you type "Smith ancient Rome" into your computer's search engine. The result is an endless list of books, articles, and web pages. Yeesh! That could take a while to sort through! Of course, you might narrow down the possibilities by typing in some more keywords. But wouldn't it be easier—and quicker—to type in the source's exact title?

You can prevent this nightmare by keeping track of your sources with a working bibliography. Your bibliography is a master guide to your sources. It's a list of each source's full title, the author's full name, and the publication information. When you start your project, set aside a sheet of paper or a computer document as your

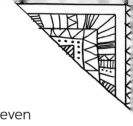

bibliography. Every time you find a new source, before you even start to take notes on it, make a bibliography entry for it. As you research, you'll add new sources. You may also cut sources that you discover you don't need after all. That's why it's called a *working* bibliography. It's still in progress.

Later, when you're going back over your notes, your bibliography will come in handy. If a note is labeled "Smith," simply check your bibliography, and you'll find all the information you need to locate the source. As a bonus, writing a working bibliography now will save you a step later, since you'll need to include a bibliography at the end of your paper. This will help your readers find your sources to learn more or to check your information.

IT'S ALL ABOUT STYLE

There is no one right way to write a bibliography for every project. That's because there are many different styles of bibliographies, and each style follows slightly different rules. Two common styles are MLA style, the style of the Modern Language Association, and APA style, the style of the American Psychological Association. Your teacher will likely tell you which style to use. Or you might have to follow the teacher's own style.

Each style requires you to list a source's information in a slightly different order, using slightly different punctuation and capitalization. And there are differences in the way you organize the information for different kinds of sources, such as books, articles, and websites.

Whoa! Are you feeling overwhelmed? Let's take a look at a few examples. You'll see that it's really not so hard!

BOOKS

Creating a bibliography entry for most books is pretty straightforward. All the information you need is usually on the title page and the copyright page (usually the back side of the title page). If no author is listed, just start with the title of the book. Here's how to put it together:

MLA

Author's last name, First name. *Title.* City: Publisher, Year. Medium of publication (print or web).

So the citation for this book would look like this:

Bodden, Valerie. *Research and Synthesize Your Facts.* Minneapolis: Lerner Publications, 2015. Print.

APA

Author's last name, Initials. (Year). *Title, with only the first word capitalized.* City, State: Publisher.

Notice the differences in how this book would be cited in APA style, compared to MLA style:

Bodden, V. (2015). *Research and synthesize your facts.* Minneapolis, MN: Lerner Publications.

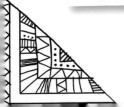

PERIODICALS

Periodicals include magazines, journals, and newspapers. You will probably find the information you need on the first page of the article and the cover of the periodical. The format for each type of periodical is slightly different, so let's take a look:

Magazine Articles

MLA

Author's last name, First name. "Title of Article." *Title of Magazine* Day Month Year: pages. Medium of publication.

Example:

Maney, Kevin. "Lose the Black Box." *Newsweek Global* 11 Apr. 2014: 1-5. Print.

APA

Author's last name, Initials. (Year, Month Day). Title of article. *Title of Magazine, volume number (issue number),* pages.

Example:

Maney, K. (2014, April 11). Lose the black box. *Newsweek Global, 162 (14),* 1-5.

Newspaper Articles

MLA

Author's last name, First name. "Title of Article." *Title of Newspaper* Day Month Year: pages. Medium of Publication.

Example:

> Trop, Jaclyn. "A Black Box for Car Crashes." *New York Times* 22 July 2013: B1-B2. Print.

APA

Author's last name, Initials. (Year, Month Day). Title of article. *Title of Newspaper*, page numbers.

Example:

> Trop, J. (2013, July 22). A black box for car crashes. *New York Times*, pp. B1-B2.

ONLINE ARTICLES

You can find many magazine, newspaper, and journal articles online too. And many websites feature articles that don't exist in print form. The citation style for articles posted online is similar to that of print articles. But instead of page numbers, you'll need to include the date you accessed the article, the publisher or sponsoring organization, and the URL (web address).

MLA

Author's last name, First name. "Title of Article." *Title of Periodical.* Publisher or Sponsoring Organization. Day Month Year. Medium of Publication. Date of Access. <URL (optional)>.

Example:

Trop, Jaclyn. "A Black Box for Car Crashes." *New York Times.* New York Times, 21 July 2013. Web. 29 Apr. 2014. <http://www.nytimes.com/2013/07/22/business/black-boxes-in-cars-a-question-of-privacy.html?_r=0>.

APA

Author's last name, Initials. (Year, Month Day). Title of article. *Title of Periodical.* Retrieved from URL

Example:

Trop, J. (2013, July 21). A black box for car crashes. *New York Times.* Retrieved from http://www.nytimes.com /2013/07/22/business/black-boxes-in-cars-a-question-of-privacy.html?_r=0

WEBSITES

Sometimes, instead of an article, you may need to cite an entire website. This can be tricky, since not all websites provide all the information you need. Find as much as you can. Check the bottom of the page for the date an article was published, for example. Or read the site's "About" page to see if you can find an author's name. If you can't find an author's name, leave it out. If you can't find a publication date, use the abbreviation n.d. to stand for no date. Let's try it!

MLA

Author's last name, first name. *Name of Site.* Name of sponsoring organization, date created or updated. Medium of publication. Date of access. <URL (optional)>.

Example:

> *American Red Cross.* American Red Cross, 2014. Web. 29 Apr. 2014. <http://www.redcross.org/>.

APA

Author's last name, Initials. (Date created or updated). *Title of document.* Retrieved from URL

Example:

> *American Red Cross.* (2014). Retrieved from http://www.redcross.org/

Note that since there is no author, the title of the website is listed first. And for MLA style, you still need to list a sponsoring organization even if it shares a name with the website.

STYLE GUIDES

Whew! Of course, this short list of examples doesn't cover all the types of sources you may need to list in your bibliography. What about interviews, films, videos, or works of art? Then there are sources with more than one author, sources with editors, and multivolume sources. The possibilities seem almost endless! How will you ever know how to cite everything? Fortunately, there are entire books dedicated to these styles, including the *MLA Handbook for Writers of Research Papers* and the *Publication Manual of the American Psychological Association.* Or you can consult online guides. With some digging, you can find out how to cite nearly any source. If you get stuck, ask your teacher for help.

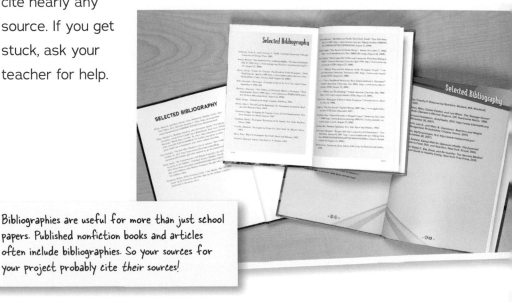

Bibliographies are useful for more than just school papers. Published nonfiction books and articles often include bibliographies. So your sources for your project probably cite their sources!

AVOIDING PLAGIARISM

Why go to all this trouble to keep track of your sources, both in your notes and in your bibliography? There are lots of reasons. For one thing, you want to give credit to the original author. After all, the author put a lot of hard work into gathering and writing the information you are using. In addition, listing your sources helps give credibility to your argument. Your readers want to know that you didn't just make all this stuff up. It also allows those readers to find more information if they're looking for it. And one of the most important reasons to cite your sources is to avoid committing plagiarism.

Plagiarism is simple enough: taking credit for someone else's work. It's illegal. You probably know that turning in a paper written by someone else and claiming that you wrote it is plagiarism. And of course, copying big chunks of someone else's paper is a no-no. But did you know that forgetting to put quotation marks around a quote is plagiarism too? So is forgetting to cite a source or paraphrasing another author's words too closely.

Yikes! It's a little scary to think you could commit plagiarism by accident. But if you're careful with your note-taking, you won't have to worry about accidentally using someone else's words as your own. That's why you need to make sure to include source information on each of your notes. If you're quoting, make sure to use quotation marks. Copy the source exactly, word for word.

If you're copying and pasting text from the Internet into your notes, take extra care to mark the text as a quotation. Consider highlighting it or changing the type color to set it apart from paraphrases and summaries. Remember, just because something is on the Internet does not mean you can use it without crediting the source.

When you're paraphrasing or summarizing, look away from your source. Think about what you've read. Then write it in your own words. You're much less likely to use the same words or sentence structure as the author if you're not looking at the source as you write. After you've made your note, double-check that the wording isn't too similar to the original text.

The penalty for plagiarism can be a failing grade or worse. It has even cost some people their careers. So learn how to avoid it now. It can save you a lot of trouble in the future.

CHAPTER 4

PUT IT ALL TOGETHER

Once you have a big stack of notes, it must be time to actually start writing your paper, right? We're so close! But first, you need to bring a little organization to your notes. That's where the outline comes in.

An outline is like a map for your paper. It helps you plan which points you will make and the order in which you will make them. Maybe you don't think you need an outline. After all, everything you need is right there, in your notes. But your information isn't organized. And that means that you're going to spend a lot of extra time trying to figure out what comes next and where to find the notes you need when you need them. With good notes, it shouldn't take you long to put together a first-rate outline and move on to the real deal.

ORGANIZING YOUR NOTES

If you're going to make a map, it helps to know where you're heading. Remember your thesis, the main point you want to prove? That's your end point. It's also your starting point. You'll use your research to complete the circle.

So how do you decide what path you'll take to prove your thesis? Start by sorting through your notes. Separate them by their subject headings. Now check how many separate subject headings you have. Ideally, you'll have three or four. That should be enough subtopics for the size of your project. If you have too many, try to group a couple of subtopics together. If you are writing about bears and have subject headings for "foraging" and "hunting prey," for example, you might group them into one category: "finding food." If you can't group your subtopics, you may need to cut one or two. It might seem painful, since you took the time to write all those notes, but it's easier to cut now than after you've written your paper. Decide which subtopic is least directly related to your thesis, and set those notes aside. (Don't throw them away yet. You may do some rethinking later and realize you can use those notes after all!)

What if you have only one or two subject headings? Go back through your notes to see if you can split one subtopic into two separate categories. Maybe you're writing about Frederick Douglass, and one of your subtopics is "antislavery activities." That's

pretty broad. You might split that category into "writing," "public speaking," and "helping escaped slaves." If your categories aren't broad enough to break apart, you may need to do more research to come up with another subtopic to support your paper.

Once you've sorted your notes, consider how the subtopics are connected. Figure out an order in which to present them. Thinking about your purpose in writing (to explain, to compare, or to persuade, for example) can help you choose the most logical way to lay out your points.

If you're discussing someone's life or an event, it may make the most sense to organize your points chronologically. If you want to show how one thing caused another, you might start with the cause and then describe the effect. Or you could start with the effect and then explain what caused it. If you are comparing and contrasting two things, you can discuss one and then the other. Or you can discuss the similarities between the two things and then the differences. If you are explaining something, you might start with the simplest information and then talk about more complex ideas. If you are discussing a problem, you might lay out how or why the problem occurs and then offer one or more solutions. For a persuasive paper, you can start with your least important argument and end with your strongest—or you might work from strongest to weakest.

If your research topic is Frederick Douglass (above), you might organize your paper chronologically.

Organize each set of notes within a subtopic, and then put those subtopics together in the order that makes the most sense. There! You've done most of the work for your outline. Now all you have to do is write it!

WRITING THE OUTLINE

Wait a minute. Isn't writing an outline complicated, with Roman numerals and letters and all kinds of rules? Well, yes, some formal outlines do use all that stuff. But once you learn how, it's not complicated. You use a Roman numeral to label each paragraph. So Roman numeral I is for your introduction, which should include your thesis. The last Roman numeral is for your conclusion, which will wrap up the points you've made and restate your thesis.

The Roman numerals in between are the body of your paper: your supporting paragraphs. Each of these paragraphs will cover a specific subtopic from your research. Capital letters indented below the Roman numerals mark the points you want to cover in each paragraph. And numbers indented under the letters list details that help prove those points: facts, examples, expert opinions, and more. Let's say you're researching active volcanoes. One of your paragraphs might be about the dangers volcanoes pose to people living near them. So it might look like this:

II. Volcanic eruptions can be dangerous for people and property nearby.
    A. Pyroclastic Flows and Explosions
        1. Hot rock and ash up to 1,300°F (704°C) can race down mountains in pyroclastic flows.
        2. Flows can spread hundreds or thousands of miles.
        3. Explosions can fling chunks of rock and debris, known as bombs.
    B. Gas Clouds and Ash Falls
    C. Avalanches, Tsunamis, and Mudslides

You could fill in more details under points B and C too. Your teacher may or may not expect you to use full sentences in your outline. Ask if you're not sure.

But what if your teacher doesn't require you to write an outline? Should you jump up and cheer? Sure! Then sit back down and write an outline anyway. You need a map to get where you're going. Since you don't need to hand in your outline, though, it doesn't need to be formal. Maybe you just want to write a list of the subtopics you will cover in the order you will cover them. You might write in a few details under each subtopic too. But you can ignore the Roman numerals and other formatting. So, if you aren't required to write a formal outline for your volcano paper, you might just write this:

Dangers of volcanoes
    -pyroclastic flows and explosions
        -temperature of flow
        -distance of flow
        -bombs
    -gas and ash
    -avalanches, tsunamis, and mudslides

It gets the same points across. And most important, it helps you plan how to make those points.

You don't need to include all of your notes in your outline. But it can be helpful to jot down where you plan to use quotes or specific sources. Then you'll be able to pull those sources out and plug them into your paper when you're writing.

CHECK FOR HOLES

OK, you're thinking there can't possibly by anything else you need to do before you start writing. And you're right—almost. But let's take one more step to make writing painless: check the outline for holes. We want to make sure that we haven't missed anything and that we're still saying what we planned to say.

Start by looking at your thesis statement. Do the points you're planning to make in the body of your paper still support your original thesis? If not, you need to tweak either the thesis or the support paragraphs. Say your original thesis was *Kids benefit from sports because they develop good health habits, confidence, and a competitive edge.* But maybe your research didn't turn up much information on developing a competitive edge through sports. Instead, you found a lot about teamwork. You can change your thesis to reflect your research: *Kids benefit from sports because they develop good health habits, confidence, and the ability to work as part of a team.* Or if you want to stick with your original thesis, you could do some more digging to find evidence on the "competitive edge" front.

And speaking of more digging, check that you have enough information to support your thesis. Do you have at least three supporting paragraphs? Do you have at least two or three points to discuss in each paragraph? What about

supporting information? Do you have statistics, examples, or quotes to help back up each point? Have you mentioned any arguments against your thesis? Do you have facts to help you refute those arguments? If the answer to any of those questions is no, go back to your sources to fill in those gaps. If you can't find information in your current sources, then search for a source that can provide the information you need. And if you can't find any information to refute the opposition's points, look for evidence that proves your thesis is still strong despite the arguments against it.

Now look at your outline one last time. Is everything in it relevant to your thesis? If something doesn't relate to your thesis, take it out—even if it's super interesting and even if you worked super hard to find it. No matter how cool it is, if it's not connected to your thesis, it will weaken your project. Maybe you're doing a report on sharks, and along the way, you learn that stingrays (relatives of sharks) produce a venom that ancient dentists used to numb their patients' mouths. It's a really cool fact—and one that you're probably eager to share. But if you include it in your paper, you'll likely confuse your readers. So cut it (and keep it in mind for the topic of your *next* research paper).

ALL ORGANIZED?

Congratulations! You're organized. Your notes are sorted, your bibliography is up to date, your outline is written, and the holes are filled. That means you are officially ready to write your paper. Now that you've put so much work into writing your map, following it should be easy.

That doesn't mean you always have to do exactly what your outline says. When you start writing, you may find that you need to change the order of some points. You might run out of room and have to cut some information. You might come up short and need to go hunting again. But by this time, you'll be so familiar with your topic and your research that these last tweaks won't trip you up. So grab your outline and your notes. Have your original sources handy in case you need to double-check something or make a last-minute addition. Settle into a comfortable chair . . . and get writing!

NOW YOU DO IT

It's time to practice taking your own notes, so grab one of your sources. First things first: make a bibliography entry for the source. Next, read the first couple of paragraphs. When you're done, look away. Write a short summary of what the author said in those paragraphs. Read the paragraphs again, and then look away and paraphrase one key idea. Look at the text one more time. This time, write a note quoting at least one sentence of the source. Don't forget to use quotation marks. Make sure all of your notes are labeled with the author's last name and the page number, as well as a subject heading. Finally, write a personal note describing your own thoughts about what you've read.

GLOSSARY

bibliography: a list of sources used in a research project

chronologically: arranged or told in order from earliest to latest or most recent

contradict: to disagree with or state the opposite of something

credibility: the quality of being believable or trustworthy

journal: a periodical about a specific subject or industry. Journal articles are often scholarly in nature.

paraphrase: to restate someone else's ideas in your own words

periodical: a publication that comes out regularly, such as once a week, once a month, or once a year

persuasive: able or intending to convince someone that a certain viewpoint is correct or to take a certain action

preliminary: an early stage of a project, or something that is not final

refute: to prove someone or something wrong

relevant: directly related to a topic or a point

thesis: a sentence that states what you will prove in your paper

SELECTED BIBLIOGRAPHY

Ballenger, Bruce. *The Curious Researcher: A Guide to Writing Research Papers*. New York: Pearson Longman, 2004.

Chin, Beverly Ann, ed. *How to Write a Great Research Paper*. San Francisco: John Wiley & Sons, 2004.

Fox, Tom, Julia Johns, and Sarah Keller. *Cite It Right*. Osterville, MA: SourceAid, 2007.

Lester, James D., Jr., and James D. Lester Sr. *Research Paper Handbook*. Tucson, AZ: Good Year Books, 2005.

Online Writing Lab. Purdue University. April 29, 2014. https://owl .english.purdue.edu/owl/resource/747/07.

Turabian, Kate. *A Manual for Writers of Research Papers, Theses, and Dissertations*. Chicago: University of Chicago Press, 2013.

FURTHER INFORMATION

Bodden, Valerie. *Write and Revise Your Project*. Minneapolis: Lerner
　　Publications, 2015. Once you have your outline completed, turn
　　to this book to learn how to write your paper.

———. *Writing a Research Paper*. Mankato, MN: Creative Education,
　　2014. Learn more about how to write a research paper from
　　start to finish.

The Kentucky Virtual Library Presents: How to Do Research
　　http://www.kyvl.org/kids/homebase.html
　　Check out the section on notes to learn more about different
　　note-taking methods and find the one that works best for you.

KidsHealth: What Is Plagiarism?
　　http://kidshealth.org/kid/feeling/school/plagiarism.html
　　Get more information on plagiarism—and how to avoid it.

Scholastic Writing Workshop: Research Paper
　　http://teacher.scholastic.com/activities/writing/minilessons
　　.asp?topic=Research
　　Get an overview of the steps needed to plan and write a
　　research paper, as well as printable worksheets to help you
　　take notes.

Time for Kids: Writing Tips
　　http://www.timeforkids.com/homework-helper/writing-tips
　　Find tips for researching and writing your paper from writers at
　　Time for Kids.

INDEX

PHOTO ACKNOWLEDGMENTS

The images in this book are used with the permission of: © Mohol/Dreamstime.com, p. 4; © iStockphoto.com/akekoksomistock, p. 5; © iStockphoto.com/futureimage, p. 6; © Todd Strand/Independent Picture Service, pp. 7, 8, 25; © iStockphoto.com/Liliboas, p. 9; © urfin/Shutterstock.com, p. 10; © iStockphoto.com/TonyBaggett, p. 11; © Julien Tromeur/Shutterstock.com, p. 12; © iStockphoto.com/gbh007, p. 14; Library of Congress LC-DIG-ds-00123, p. 15; NASA, p. 16; © iStockphoto.com/PaulFleet, p. 18; © iStockphoto.com/hudiemm, p. 20; © iStockphoto.com/NatashaBo, p. 21; © Feng Yu/Shutterstock.com, p. 22; © iStockphoto.com/ollo, p. 26; © iStockphoto.com/paulw11, p. 27; © iStockphoto.com/stuartbur, p. 28 (top); © iStockphoto.com/3dfoto, p. 28 (bottom); © iStockphoto.com/GlobalP, p. 29; Library of Congress LC-USZ62-15887, p. 30; © Fuse/Thinkstock, p. 31; © CoreyFord/iStock/Thinkstock, p. 32; © iStockphoto.com/CEFutcher, p. 34.

Cover and interior backgrounds: © koosen/Shutterstock (brown background); © Mrs. Opossum/Shutterstock (zig zag pattern); © AKSANA SHUM/Shutterstock (diamond pattern); © AtthameeNi/Shutterstock (blue lined graph paper); © Looper/Shutterstock (arrows); © AlexanderZam/Shutterstock (graph paper dots); © oleschwander/Shutterstock (yellow lined paper dots).